LEADING IS TEACHING

Jesus' Model for Developing Others

John W. Stanko

Leading is Teaching
by John W. Stanko
Copyright ©2025 John W. Stanko

ISBN 978-1-63360-343-1

All rights reserved. This book is protected under the copyright laws of the United States of America. This book may not be copied or reprinted for com-mercial gain or profit.

Scripture quotations are taken from THE HOLY BIBLE: New International Version ©1978 by the New York International Bible Society, used by permission of Zondervan Bible Publishers. All rights reserved.

       For Worldwide Distribution   Printed in the USA

Urban Press
PO Box 5044
Williamsburg, VA 23188
757.808.5776
www.urbanpress.us

Introduction	v

Section One
Leaders and the Seven Woes of Matthew 23

chapter 1 **Teaching and Leading**	3
chapter 2 **The First Woe - Shutting the Door**	11
chapter 3 **The Second Woe - Misguided Efforts**	17
chapter 4 **The Third Woe - Starting Points**	24
chapter 5 **The Fourth Woe - Justice, Mercy, Faithfulness**	30
chapter 6 **The Fifth Woe - Kiss or Miss**	36
chapter 7 **The Sixth Woe - Whitewashed Tombs**	42
chapter 8 **The Seventh Woe - Talk is Cheap**	48

Section Two
Teaching as a Path to Servant Leadership

chapter 9 **Moses' Seat**	55
chapter 10 **Humility**	67
chapter 11 **Good Guides**	75
chapter 12 **Jesus Came to Serve**	89
epilogue **Servant Leadership - Teaching as the Heart of Influence**	104

Introduction

The writings of Robert Greenleaf, who coined the phrase "servant leader," have held my attention and molded my leadership philosophy for many years. I've read and re-read most of his servant leader essays and books that first piqued my interest in 1998. Of course, I have taken his insights to the word of God to receive even more understanding (or adjustment) as to what it means to be a servant leader.

Who This Book Is For

This book is written for anyone who leads or influences others—whether in a church, business, nonprofit, educational, or community setting. If you find yourself guiding people, teaching, mentoring, or managing teams, this book is for you. It is especially relevant to:

- Pastors, ministry leaders, and church volunteers who desire to lead as Jesus taught, embodying servant leadership and teaching as inseparable callings.
- Educators and teachers who want to serve their students well, helping them grow not just in knowledge but in character and purpose.

- Business leaders, managers, and team leaders committed to fostering growth and development in their organizations through humility, service, and effective teaching and training.
- Anyone who feels called to make a difference by empowering others, whether formally or informally.

In all these roles, the challenge is the same: to lead not by position or title, but by serving others, teaching with integrity, and modeling the life-transforming love of Christ. This book offers insights, biblical examples, and practical applications to help you grow in this vital leadership role.

Robert Greenleaf was a Quaker, but his writings are for the most part devoid of biblical references. The foundation for some of his teaching was the writing of Hermann Hesse, an author whose work contained Buddhist overtones. This has caused some people of faith to ignore or even oppose Greenleaf's message, but I'm not one of them. That's because I hold to the fact that all truth is God's truth. All the Bible is true but not all truth is in the Bible. I've spent a good part of my adult life evaluating Greenleaf's principles according to biblical guidelines, and have found many of them to be sound and consistent, even though Greenleaf was not using the Bible as a reference as far as I know.

This was brought home to me in Indonesia when I was there consulting with a large group of bankers and land developers. Indonesia is a Muslim country and I was not permitted to reference faith or the Bible unless I was asked about it. When I was teaching about servant leadership, a man in the audience raised his hand and asked, "Wasn't Jesus a servant leader?" With that opening, I proceeded to share stories of Jesus' teaching and ministry, showing that the servant leader message didn't begin with Greenleaf; it started with and was modeled by Jesus.

> Then they began to argue among themselves about who would be the greatest among them. Jesus told them, "In this world the kings and great men lord it over their people, yet they are called 'friends of the people.' But among you it will be different. Those who are the greatest among you should take the lowest rank, and the leader should be like a servant. Who is more important, the one who sits at the table or the one who serves? The one who sits at the table, of course. But not here! For I am among you as one who serves" (Luke 22:24-27).

It's therefore surprising that I have never heard a message taught in a church setting that focused on leaders as servants. Perhaps I simply haven't found the right source, but I've been looking for it—somewhere, anywhere, from anyone. That being said, I've read just about anything I could find from other authors who wrote or talked about servant leadership. They also did not usually approach the subject from a biblical worldview.

However, I still found what they wrote

valuable in that it provided a different perspective for me to consider. I used what they wrote to learn more, incorporating some of their work in my lectures and writing. As long as what they wrote did not contradict Scripture, I felt free to use it. I'm going to share some of what I learned with you in this book. I invite you, if you are a person of faith, to do what I did: judge the content based on biblical principles and not by the source of who wrote or taught it—or the means used to prove their point.

My studies and writing opened doors for me to teach in various settings—universities, churches, conferences—and now I am an author and publisher of both books and digital and social media content. Because of the opportunities that technology provides, I find myself in the role of a teacher more than ever before. This motivated me to study not only the role of servant leaders but also the role of a teacher in the Bible, while also accessing and applying the best educational techniques and strategies I could find. My studies and teaching career have yielded much fruit and contributed greatly to my ongoing "infatuation" with servant-leadership concepts. I feel that now is the time to share with you what I have been learning.

Jesus was both the consummate servant and teacher in His leadership role. His followers and associates called him "rabbi" or "teacher," and it seems that Jesus expected all His followers to teach at some point in time. One of His last commands on earth can be found in Matthew 28:19-20:

> "Therefore go and make disciples of all nations, baptizing them in the name of the Father and of the Son and of the Holy Spirit, and teaching them to obey everything I have commanded you. And surely I am with you always, to the very end of the age" (emphasis added).

The writer of Hebrews (and it's my opinion that it was the Apostle Paul who at least collaborated on the letter) wrote,

> In fact, though by this time you ought to be teachers, you need someone to teach you the elementary truths of God's word all over again. You need milk, not solid food! (Hebrews 5:12).

I conclude that the lessons we can learn about effective teaching applies not only to those who officially function in a teaching role, but to all of us, whether we are teaching our children, grandchildren, volunteers, or employees in a business or ministry setting. In other words, the lessons we can learn about servant leadership from a teacher's perspective are applicable to all of us, and that includes you—yes, you.

The world right now is filled with leaders who are anything but servants. We're suffering the effects of a leadership crisis in society and that includes the Church, yet we keep right on doing the same things, somehow expecting better or different results. We are plagued with ineffective leadership, which means the practice of servant leadership is

Leading is Teaching

more needed than ever—even though I see it discussed less and less in recent years in business or academic circles. I shouldn't be surprised, for a world consumed with the pursuit of power and wealth is not the best seedbed for things like humility, listening, and persuasion—all traits vital to the servant leader.

I invite you to come along with me in the following pages as we look at stories of Jesus when He taught. Of particular interest to us will be His words in Matthew 23 where He castigated the leaders of Israel for their approach to leadership. It was in this context that we find the seven "woes" that Jesus pronounced to those leader. We will examine those woes to see what we can learn about teaching and leadership—and how the two flow together.

Regardless of what and from whom we are learning about leadership, Jesus should be our ultimate model. He was the best leader and teacher the world has ever seen. I don't want to pattern my leadership or teaching after anyone else but Him, and He is ultimately the one I must please in either role. I hope you can say the same, and toward that end, let's work together to make it happen to the glory of God as we go through *Leading Is Teaching: Jesus' Model for Developing Others* **together.**

John W. Stanko
Pittsburgh, PA
December 2025

SECTION ONE

**LEADERS
AND THE SEVEN WOES
OF MATTHEW 23**

chapter 1

Teaching and Leading

Let's start with Jesus' words to the leadership of Israel found in Matthew 23. During His sermon, Jesus identified seven leadership problems and offered practical examples of their "woeful" leadership to illustrate His points. What can we learn from His encounter with these leaders? Isn't there a world of difference between the challenges faced during Jesus' world and those of the modern day?

Actually, there isn't that much difference. People are the same today as they were then. Leaders face the same temptations—money, sex, and power. Our sin problem affected leadership attitudes and decisions then just like it does now, so studying the leadership problem using Jesus' own words is an important, although sometimes neglected, thing to do.

As stated in the Introduction, there's a leadership crisis in the Church (and in society for that matter), so anything we can do to contribute to leadership growth and improvement will go a long way toward addressing the crisis. Let's begin our discussion with Jesus' preamble leading up to the woes:

> Then Jesus said to the crowds and to his disciples: "The teachers of the law and the Pharisees sit in Moses' seat. So you must be careful to do everything they tell you. But do not do what they do, for they do not practice what they preach. They tie up heavy, cumbersome loads and put them on other people's shoulders, but they themselves are not willing to lift a finger to move them.
>
> "But you are not to be called 'Rabbi,' for you have one Teacher, and you are all brothers. And do not call anyone on earth 'father,' for you have one Father, and he is in heaven. Nor are you to be called instructors, for you have one Instructor, the Messiah. The greatest among you will be your servant. For those who exalt themselves will be humbled, and those who humble themselves will be exalted" (Matthew 23:1-12).

Rather than look at the negatives of what the leaders were not doing, let's determine what they should have been doing so we can adopt and develop those behaviors and attitudes:

1. **Leaders must practice what they preach.** We can't take people where we're not willing to go ourselves, both externally and internally.

2. **Leaders must help people carry their burdens.** That means we must be careful not to become an additional burden to our followers.
3. **Leaders must do things not just to be seen or heard.** We should make a beneficial difference in the lives of others, doing it for the Lord who will reward us.
4. **Leaders should do all they can to blend in with the people.** We should not set ourselves apart by where we sit, what we wear, or how we are treated and addressed.
5. **Leaders, whether in church or business, are simply members or employees who have a leadership role.** This doesn't make us special or warrant favored treatment. Seeking after titles or allowing people to assign those titles is discouraged, if not strictly forbidden.

The benefit and drawback often lies in how leadership relates to the issue of power, which automatically comes with any leadership position. Even a teacher who is leading a class has power: power to teach whatever they choose, to structure the class as they think best, to engage with the students or not, and, in school settings, the power to pass or fail.

When you were in school, you encountered teachers. Some of them you liked and some you didn't. The ones you liked knew their material, and they were accessible. You got the sense they were learning right along with you. They didn't mind questions, but they also kept a firm hand on the direction of the class. And they probably had your best interests at heart.

The ones you didn't relate to as well were those who may have known their material, but their attitude was poor. They were aloof, insecure, and paid little attention to the students. They were going to get through their material come heaven or high water, and the students were privileged to be along for the ride. You may even encounter some of this now with someone who teaches from a church pulpit.

What was the problem? Why could you relate better to some than others? The problem was and is power and how they used or misused it. When our fallen nature catches a whiff of power, no matter the position we hold, it can be intoxicating. If leaders haven't prepared themselves for that power and its potential effects, it can be detrimental—to them and their followers. The only antidote I have found for the negative effects of leadership power is serving others—taking the power leaders have and using it to empower others for learning and success. Otherwise, the leaders will use their power to build their own kingdom and not God's, regardless of whether they are leading in the Church or not.

The teachers you liked, or who were most effective, used their power not to dominate the class, but to lead it. They were good listeners and were there to help you learn, willing to do whatever they could to facilitate that process. They were not a sage from the stage, but rather a guide from the side. They may have demanded more from you than you thought you could produce, but you learned because you wanted to, not because you had to.

And the same is probably true for those leaders you admired and wanted to follow. You never got the idea it was about them, but about the mission and about those they were leading—and the Lord if they were His followers. They served others to help them not only do the work but also develop and grow.

There's much more in those Matthew 23 verses and as you read them you may think, *Amen!* Some leaders and teachers may even come to mind as you read. Yet the practice of overbearing pastors, armor-bearers, special seating, and titles, along with lack of service practiced by leaders, continue to plague the Church (and business) despite Jesus' teachings and warnings. We accept that as normal because that's the tradition of our church or denomination and we don't stop to think about, evaluate, and then change what we have done or do. We expect leaders to lead but we usually don't see or think of them as servants in their leadership roles.

I urge you to examine your own heart where these issues are concerned and not be ready to judge others until you have dealt with these matters yourself. I have found if you don't prepare for leadership power before you have it, it is certain to overwhelm and mislead you when you do. And it's easy to judge a leader but a bit more difficult when you have faced your own temptation to misuse leadership power.

What's more, don't assume you are a servant or even know how to serve. Don't criticize others who do things to be noticed until you stop doing so yourself, or at least are no longer offended when you aren't recognized for your service and good deeds. Decide and then prepare for what kind of leader you're going to be *before* you access and utilize leadership power.

Leadership isn't second nature to most of us. By that, I mean that when you become a leader, you won't know how to lead unless you have studied leadership as a practice. You may be an effective doctor or theologian, but that doesn't mean you are equipped to lead when the opportunity arises. And once you lead, you must continue to learn and develop, otherwise the office and title will beguile you into thinking that you earned them because you're special. Once again, the only practice that will keep your leadership grounded in humility and grace is servant leadership.

Now let's take a look at the seven woes, devoting a chapter to each one of them. Then in the next section we are going to examine those same verses to see what they can teach us about the role of a teacher and how it can naturally partner with the role of a servant leader.

Summary Points

- Leadership and teaching are closely connected callings that reflect the heart of Jesus' example.
- Traditional leadership models often emphasize authority and control, but servant leadership calls for humility, serice, and nurturing growth.
- Effective leaders recognize that teaching others is a vital part of their role.
- This section sets the stage for exploring servant leadership's practical outworking in various contexts.
- You are invited to prepare your heart and mind for a journey of transformation toward servant-teaching leadership.

Reflection Questions

1. What assumptions about leadership have you held that this section challenges?
2. How does the idea of leadership as teaching resonate with your experience or calling?
3. In what ways do you currently serve those you lead or influence?
4. What fears or barriers do you face in adopting a servant-leadership approach?
5. How can you prepare yourself to grow as both a servant and a teacher in your leadership journey?

chapter 2

The First Woe— Shutting the Door

In Chapter One, I pointed out that Jesus' message to the leadership in Matthew 23 contained seven warnings, all marked by the word "woe." Woe is a term that designates sadness or doom and is in stark contrast to the words "blessed" or "happy" that Jesus used when He began His public ministry: "Blessed [happy] are the poor in spirit, for theirs is the kingdom of heaven" (Matthew 5:3). Let's examine the reason for the first woe and see what the leaders were doing that attracted God's anger (so we can learn to avoid the same behavior):

> "Woe to you, teachers of the law and Pharisees, you hypocrites! You shut the door of the kingdom of heaven in people's faces. You yourselves do not enter, nor will you let those enter who are trying to" (Matthew 23:13-14).

Here are some thoughts on this first woe:

1. The leaders were hypocrites who were wearing a mask, pretending to be righteous when they were not. They had deceived themselves that they actually were righteous and in right standing with God. God requires us to be honest about who we are, seek Him for internal transformation in the power of the Spirit, and then act in a way consistent with those internal changes.
2. The leaders couldn't take people to a good place because they had never gone there themselves. We can't reproduce in the lives of others what we haven't partnered with God to produce in ourselves.
3. The goal or destination was the Kingdom of heaven, not the kingdom of men or religion. If the "rules" of God aren't the main focus, we tend to create our own rules and they're usually harsher than God's.
4. Not only were the leaders not in touch with God's kingdom requirements, they were slamming the door in the faces of those who wanted to know God's will for their lives. (It's considered rude to slam the door in someone's face and non-servant leaders can often be rude people.) This tells us that we as leaders are to help people

know and do God's will for their lives. When we don't do that, followers are stymied in their spiritual or professional progress.

This clearly indicates that Jesus expects any leader, in the church or outside it, to assist others to fulfill their purpose in the Lord by taking the things they (the leaders) have learned and helping others learn from those experiences. Leaders are to be accessible and willing to assist others not as experts (even though they may be) but rather as fellow seekers and disciples. This process is best summarized by what Peter wrote in his epistle:

> Be shepherds of God's flock that is under your care, watching over them—not because you must, but because you are willing, as God wants you to be; not pursuing dishonest gain, but eager to serve; not lording it over those entrusted to you, but being examples to the flock. And when the Chief Shepherd appears, you will receive the crown of glory that will never fade away (1 Peter 5:2-4).

Peter indicated that the attitude of leaders must be that they lead 1) willingly; 2) to serve and not to amass wealth; and 3) as role models and not as autocrats. It's obvious that the Pharisees' and Sadducees' attitudes were the exact opposite. They served the people grudgingly and with cruelty, did it for money and prestige, and used their positional power to lord their authority over others.

What kind of a leader are you? Are you a door opener for others or a door slammer? Do you serve or lord? Are you growing or expecting others to grow while you stagnate or regress? You will see clearly in this book that Jesus expects His leaders to differ from those found in the world. He doesn't apologize for His expectations, and what's more, He modeled them firsthand for us to see and emulate. Let's make sure we adopt the correct standards when we evaluate our leadership or that of others, otherwise we may be walking the valley of woe that's the destination for any leader who refuses to adopt God's leadership ways.

Summary Points

- Servant leadership is grounded in the example and teachings of Jesus, who called leaders to serve rather than dominate.
- Robert Greenleaf's concept of the servant leader emphasizes leadership as a calling to serve and develop others with humility and love.
- True leadership involves teaching—not just directing—helping others grow in character, faith, and purpose.
- Leadership isn't limited to church settings but applies across business, education, nonprofit, and community contexts.
- The challenge of leadership is to lead by serving, modeling Christlike love and integrity in all areas of influence.

Reflection Questions

1. How do you currently understand your role as a leader or teacher? Is serving a visible part of that role?
2. In what ways have you seen leadership succeed or fail when teaching and serving are absent?
3. Reflect on a leader or teacher in your life who embodied servant leadership. What made their leadership effective?
4. What specific challenges do you face in your leadership or teaching role that this chapter's insights might help you address?
5. How can you better integrate teaching and serving in your leadership to reflect the example of Jesus?

chapter 3

The Second Woe— Misguided Efforts

Let's look at the second woe and see what we can learn and apply to our own leadership and teaching philosophy:

> "Woe to you, teachers of the law and Pharisees, you hypocrites! You travel over land and sea to win a single convert, and when you have succeeded, you make them twice as much a child of hell as you are" (Matthew 23:15).

Paul summarized the problem with the leaders of his people when he wrote, "For I can testify about them that they are zealous for God, but their zeal is not based on knowledge" (Romans 10:2). God expects His leaders to focus on the important things— His priorities—and build His kingdom, not their own. The leaders in Jesus' day were doing the opposite.

What's more, because they hadn't achieved any spiritual maturity themselves, they were incapable of leading anyone to a better place in the Lord. Therefore, their converts were actually further removed from the spiritual reality they so desperately needed, and thus incapable of entering into a healthy spiritual place.

In modern terms, we often label someone who travels to recruit followers to a particular belief as an evangelist. Jesus indicated in this second woe that there were Jewish evangelists who traveled for the sole purpose of gaining converts to Judaism. My personal theory is that Saul was such a man. When someone needed to go to Damascus to hunt down and persecute believers (see Acts 9), Saul volunteered to go because he had been there before—or at least wasn't intimidated to go.

No member of the Sanhedrin wanted to go to a Gentile land for fear of becoming unclean, but Saul had no such fear because he knew how to travel and stay undefiled. He had probably been to Damascus (and other cities) to further Jewish interests but the Lord apprehended him to confront him with the reality of woe number two (remember, this is my theory). Saul was making his converts twice the son of hell that he was, but then became an evangelist who set people free in Christ rather than burdening them with useless traditions—and poor leadership.

God expects His leaders not to bind up followers under legalistic rituals and rules that limit their creativity and growth. They must teach followers how to apply general principles to the new challenges every generation must face so the Lord is honored and His purpose served and enhanced. This includes denominations and faith-based organizations that delight in having their adherents follow the traditions they have honed over time rather than a life of the Spirit who leads and guides His followers into all the truth.

In other words, God's leaders are to be people of wisdom who impart wisdom to others. Paul told us what, or rather who, wisdom is:

> But we preach Christ crucified: a stumbling block to Jews and foolishness to Gentiles, but to those whom God has called, both Jews and Greeks, Christ the power of God and the wisdom of God. For the foolishness of God is wiser than human wisdom, and the weakness of God is stronger than human strength (1 Corinthians 1:23-25).

> My goal is that they may be encouraged in heart and united in love, so that they may have the full riches of complete understanding, in order that they may know the mystery of God, namely, Christ, in whom are hidden all the treasures of wisdom and knowledge. I tell you this so that no one may deceive you by fine-sounding arguments (Colossians 2:2-4).

Our wisdom isn't a body of knowledge, but rather a person. Therefore, if we're going to be godly leaders and teachers, we must connect our students and followers to the source and embodiment of wisdom, which is Christ. And what should this wisdom equip the listeners to do? It shouldn't help them perpetuate a past that's no longer functional, but rather to create a future that will enable people to fulfill their creative purpose in changing times.

I encourage you to read Proverbs 8 in its entirety, but here are two excerpts from what the wisdom writer told us about wisdom:

> "By me kings reign and rulers issue decrees that are just; by me princes govern, and nobles—all who rule on earth. I love those who love me, and those who seek me find me. With me are riches and honor, enduring wealth and prosperity. My fruit is better than fine gold; what I yield surpasses choice silver" (Proverbs 8:15-19).

> "Now then, my children, listen to me; blessed are those who keep my ways. Listen to my instruction and be wise; do not disregard it. ... Blessed are those who listen to me, watching daily at my doors, waiting at my doorway. For those who find me find life and receive favor from the Lord. But those who fail to find me harm themselves; all who hate me love death" (Proverbs 8:32-36).

What kind of leader are you? Are you setting people free or binding them up? Are you giving them godly wisdom or teaching them the ways of dead or dying traditions? Don't answer too quickly, but instead seek the Lord to help you understand what kind of "evangelist" you are—one who recruits people to a life of freedom and wisdom or to a life of bondage to dead works.

Summary Points

- Recognizing the pitfalls Jesus highlighted in Matthew 23 helps leaders avoid common errors such as hypocrisy, pride, and legalism.
- Authentic servant leadership requires self-awareness and a commitment to integrity, humility, and genuine care for those led.
- Leadership isn't about external appearances or rigid rules, but about the heart's posture and consistent alignment with Christ's example.
- Leaders must cultivate an environment where teaching and learning flourish, fostering spiritual growth and maturity.
- Avoiding the "woes" Jesus spoke of is essential for effective, transformative leadership in any setting.

Reflection Questions

1. Which of the "woes" Jesus pronounced do you see most often in leadership today—and why is that?
2. How can you guard yourself against the temptation to lead with pride or hypocrisy?
3. What steps can you take to cultivate humility and integrity in your leadership?
4. In what ways can your leadership create a safe space for learning and growth?
5. How do you measure your success as a leader beyond outward accomplishments or appearances.

chapter 4

The Third Woe— Starting Points

Now let's examine the third woe Jesus listed in his sermon found in Matthew 23, and he gave more in the way of explanation for this one than for any of the others:

> "Woe to you, blind guides! You say, 'If anyone swears by the temple, it means nothing; but anyone who swears by the gold of the temple is bound by that oath.' You blind fools! Which is greater: the gold, or the temple that makes the gold sacred? You also say, 'If anyone swears by the altar, it means nothing; but anyone who swears by the gift on the altar is bound by that oath.' You blind men! Which is greater: the gift, or the altar that makes the gift sacred? Therefore, anyone who swears by the altar swears by it and by everything on it. And anyone who swears by the temple

swears by it and by the one who dwells in it. And anyone who swears by heaven swears by God's throne and by the one who sits on it" (Matthew 23:16-22).

Jesus attempted to show the leaders they were majoring in minors by emphasizing and teaching principles that seemed spiritual but were not. What does this tell us about God's expectations for leaders in and out of the church?

- God is the source of authoritative teaching on what is right and what is wrong. That source was embodied in Jesus, whom the leaders were contradicting and rejecting.
- God holds *all* leaders *everywhere* accountable to obey His words and commands. The prophets did not only address Israel but also all the surrounding nations.

Teachers and leaders must be able to learn principles and then properly apply them to real-life situations that aren't specifically addressed by those principles. For example, some aspects of modern life aren't specifically mentioned in the Bible, things like church facilities and sports, or issues like euthanasia, transgender lifestyles, or gay marriage. God expects His leaders to address those modern aspects with ancient and timeless guidance from His Word.

Jesus labeled the leaders blind (three times in this passage) and had said earlier in Matthew's gospel, "Leave them; they are blind guides. If the blind lead the blind, both will fall into a pit" (Matthew 15:14). If leaders can't see where they're going for themselves, they can't lead others to a good place.

Leaders must constantly study to hone their discernment and develop and apply wisdom, so the Jewish leaders were correct in gathering and studying regularly. But their blindness caused them to study the wrong things and/or come to the wrong conclusions. This points out the importance for all leaders to consistently challenge their "starting points" to ensure they are starting from the right logical point. Let me explain what I mean.

As one example, a Jewish leader's "starting point" was that God would never use a man to heal others on the Sabbath. Of this they were certain and used the Scriptures to justify their position. When Jesus healed, they logically concluded from an incorrect starting point that He wasn't from God and had to be executed. Even though they saw Jesus do miraculous works, their starting point caused them to misinterpret His works, and actually sentence Him to death for doing them on the "wrong" day.

In this third woe, the leaders were doing the same thing: starting at the wrong point and then traveling down the wrong path that led to erroneous conclusions. Their conclusions were logical but flawed because of their incorrect starting assumption and premise.

Do you challenge your starting points to

ensure you're starting your logic and leadership from the correct place? Are you growing and learning how to apply past experiences and ancient wisdom to daily problems you face? Who do you have in your circle of influence who challenges your thinking, starting points, assumptions, and conclusions? Are you willing and able to change your starting points so that you don't lead people astray?

If you're willing, then you'll avoid the trap of majoring in minors, emphasizing what seems important to you but isn't important to Him. That will enable you to impart life to others and not confuse them or cause them to also major in unimportant issues that seem spiritual but only lead to folly.

Summary Points

- Servant leadership requires leaders to "major in the majors"—focusing on what truly matters rather than getting caught up in trivial or secondary issues.

- Jesus criticized leaders who "shut the door of the kingdom" to others by overemphasizing rules and traditions that exclude rather than include.

- True leaders prioritize people's spiritual growth and well-being over legalism and control.

- Leadership demands discernment to balance tradition and innovation in ways that serve God's purposes and people's needs.

- Effective servant leaders continually evaluate their priorities to ensure they are aligned with Christ's heart for justice, mercy, and humility.

Reflection Questions

1. What are some "minor" issues or traditions that might be distracting you or your organization from your core mission?

2. How do you respond when confronted with legalism or exclusivity in leadership or teaching?

3. In what ways can you open "doors" rather than shut them in your leadership practice?

4. How can you balance honoring tradition with the need for grace and inclusion?

5. What steps can you take to focus more on what truly matters in your leadership or teaching role?

chapter 5

The Fourth Woe— Justice, Mercy, Faithfulness

As we continue looking at the list of "woes" Jesus presented in Matthew 23, we come to Jesus' fourth admonition as found in Matthew 23:23-24:

> "Woe to you, teachers of the law and Pharisees, you hypocrites! You give a tenth of your spices—mint, dill and cumin. But you have neglected the more important matters of the law—justice, mercy and faithfulness. You should have practiced the latter, without neglecting the former. You blind guides! You strain out a gnat but swallow a camel."

These leaders had overextended the Law to apply to irrelevant matters, or as I wrote in the last chapter, they were majoring in minors. Their hollow ritualism caused them to be blind to weightier matters that, according to Jesus, were the concepts important to God—justice, mercy, and faithfulness.

Before we condemn these men too quickly, do we have any traditions that also major in minors? How about the practice of armor bearers that some leaders deploy in the church? Or how about the attachment to titles like author, apostle, prophet, deacon, boss, or chief? Or how about corner offices and special eating places for leaders and cubicles and vending machine food for "lesser lights"? And even the more high church, liturgical churches have a plethora of "traditions" that are simply rituals void of spiritual power. Every culture has bestowed certain perks on its leaders, but do those perks contribute to justice, mercy, or faithfulness? If not, then perhaps Jesus is speaking to us as well?

Justice, mercy, and faithfulness—those words and concepts are subjective and mean something different to everyone. If I mention justice, what does it cause you to envision? For some, it's feeding the poor, for others it's education, and for still others, it may mean environmental sensitivities or equal opportunity housing. How can we come to a definition upon which we all can agree? One way would be to see what Jesus' definition was and submit to that, so let's try and do that by looking at a question someone asked Jesus:

> "Teacher, which is the greatest commandment in the Law?" Jesus replied: "'Love the Lord your God with all your heart and with all your soul and with all your mind.'

This is the first and greatest commandment. And the second is like it: 'Love your neighbor as yourself.' All the Law and the Prophets hang on these two commandments" (Matthew 22:36-40).

The first part of the definition for justice is to love God and the second is to love your neighbor as yourself. How should the second part play out in our lives? Jesus answered that in Matthew 7:12: "So in everything, do to others what you would have them do to you, for this sums up the Law and the Prophets." The Law and prophets both hang on and are summed up by loving your neighbor as yourself.

Justice and mercy are therefore to be faithfully expressed according to what you would want others to do to and for you. It's not about the church feeding more people; it's about *you* feeding more people. It's not about the government doing more for children; it's about *you* doing more for children. Then when you lead an organization or movement or speak to people in power, you can influence that group from a position of integrity and faith because you have done not what you are demanding or expecting others to do but what you have already been faithfully doing.

How do you present yourself with justice and mercy through social media? By treating others as you would want to be treated. How do you present yourself with justice and mercy to the church or government? By asking them to help you do what you're already doing to express justice and mercy, but not demanding they do it in your place.

Do you have any traditions, ways of thinking, or pet peeves that are blinding you to the need for justice, mercy, and faithfulness in your life? Are you majoring in minors? Are you self-righteous like those people Jesus was addressing in Matthew 23? Don't answer too quickly, for you may be blinded to the reality of your own heart, just like the leaders in Jesus' day were. Instead, ask the Lord to show you where you lack justice, mercy, and/or faithfulness and then seek to correct your own approach to those matters before you try and correct someone else.

Summary Points

- True servant leadership calls leaders to be authentic guides who lead by example, walking alongside those they serve.
- Jesus modeled leadership as a relational journey, not a distant or authoritarian position.
- Effective leaders invest personally in the growth and well-being of those they lead, nurturing trust and openness.
- Leadership is a daily commitment to humility, service, and teaching in the context of real relationships.
- Being a good guide means helping others navigate both challenges and opportunities with compassion and wisdom.

Reflection Questions

1. How do you currently build trust and connection with those you lead or teach?

2. In what ways can you be more present and engaged as a guide in your leadership?

3. What are the challenges of leading relationally rather than from a position of authority?

4. How can you balance the need for guidance with allowing others to take responsibility for their growth?

5. What practical steps can you take to model servant leadership more consistently in your daily interactions?

chapter 6

The Fifth Woe — Kiss or Miss

Jesus criticized the leaders of Israel in Matthew 23, pronouncing seven "woes" that summarized His complaints against them. Jesus was still reaching out to them through strong words, hoping that they would come to their senses and repent, but alas, they were too far gone to hear what He was saying. We must take His words to heart today in order to avoid the mistakes those leaders made. In His fifth woe, Jesus said,

> "Woe to you, teachers of the law and Pharisees, you hypocrites! You clean the outside of the cup and dish, but inside they are full of greed and self-indulgence. Blind Pharisee! First clean the inside of the cup and dish, and then the outside also will be clean" (Matthew 23:25-26).

What was the main problem represented in this woe? It seems that it was the mistake of emphasizing external appearance as opposed to internal substance. Jesus gave examples of this problem at other times:

> "Nothing outside a person can defile them by going into them. Rather, it is what comes out of a person that defiles them." After he had left the crowd and entered the house, his disciples asked him about this parable. "Are you so dull?" he asked. "Don't you see that nothing that enters a person from the outside can defile them? For it doesn't go into their heart but into their stomach, and then out of the body." (In saying this, Jesus declared all foods clean.) He went on: "What comes out of a person is what defiles them. For it is from within, out of a person's heart, that evil thoughts come—sexual immorality, theft, murder, adultery, greed, malice, deceit, lewdness, envy, slander, arrogance and folly. All these evils come from inside and defile a person" (Mark 7:15-23).

> "But be on your guard against the yeast of the Pharisees and Sadducees." Then they understood that he was not telling them to guard against the yeast used in bread, but against the teaching of the Pharisees and Sadducees (Matthew 16:11b-12).

Of course, Jesus modeled the behavior He expected in His leaders, which was the exact opposite of what He was describing where the leaders of

His day were concerned. Isaiah predicted this about Jesus: "He grew up before him like a tender shoot, and like a root out of dry ground. He had no beauty or majesty to attract us to him, nothing in his appearance that we should desire him" (Isaiah 53:2). Jesus had no armor bearers, no badge of honor, or no trappings of leadership that the people of His time had come to expect.

In fact, when Judas betrayed Jesus, he was concerned that the guards he was leading to Jesus wouldn't recognize Him because the Romans and Temple guards were used to their leaders standing out by their uniform or some other external distinction. Judas in essence said, "You'd better let me kiss Him or you'll miss Him!" The guards would have arrested Peter or John or any other of the disciples because Jesus wouldn't have stood out as the leader. Jesus' message is clear to His leaders: Don't work on the external trappings of power; work on the heart. He made it clear at the Last Supper how we are to do this as we saw in the Introduction:

> "But you are not to be like that. Instead, the greatest among you should be like the youngest, and the one who rules like the one who serves. For who is greater, the one who is at the table or the one who serves? Is it not the one who is at the table? But I am among you as one who serves" (Luke 22:26-27).

What are you working on to enhance your leadership? Is it the inner person of the heart? Or are you enamored with the outward benefits of leadership—the respect, the special honor, the perks like a corner office or other special benefits? Be careful, for you may begin to think you deserve those things when they're available to you, which can lead to the self-indulgence and greed that Jesus identified in the fifth woe. The only antidote for the negative effects of leadership power is service, and that service requires a humble heart that focuses on the welfare of other people.

Summary Points

- Servant leaders prioritize humility and teachability, recognizing their own need for continual growth.
- Jesus exemplified a posture of learning and dependence on the Father, modeling humility even as the ultimate leader.
- Leadership that resists pride and embraces vulnerability fosters genuine community and effective teaching.
- Servant leadership involves being open to correction and willing to adapt in response to God's guidance and others' needs.
- Cultivating a humble heart is essential to leading others toward maturity and faithfulness.

Reflection Questions

1. How do you demonstrate humility in your leadership or teaching role?

2. In what ways do you remain teachable and open to correction?

3. What challenges do you face in embracing vulnerability as a leader?

4. How can humility improve the learning environment you create for others?

5. What spiritual practices help you cultivate a humble and teachable heart?

chapter 7

The Sixth Woe—
Whitewashed Tombs

We are almost finished with our look at the woes that Jesus delivered in Matthew 23. In this lesson, we look at the next-to-the-last entry, this one found in Matthew 23:27-28:

> "Woe to you, teachers of the law and Pharisees, you hypocrites! You are like whitewashed tombs, which look beautiful on the outside but on the inside are full of the bones of the dead and everything unclean. In the same way, on the outside you appear to people as righteous but on the inside you are full of hypocrisy and wickedness."

In the previous lesson on the fifth woe, we saw how the leaders were more interested in cleaning the outside of the cup, so to speak, while ignoring cleansing the inside, which was more important in God's eyes. This woe continues with that theme.

The problem with this woe is that people were coming into contact with the leaders and there was no benefit for them when they did.

Jews weren't permitted to come into contact with a dead body or else they were rendered ceremonially unclean, which meant they couldn't participate in Temple worship or sacrifices:

> "Whoever touches a human corpse will be unclean for seven days. They must purify themselves with the water on the third day and on the seventh day; then they will be clean. But if they do not purify themselves on the third and seventh days, they will not be clean. If they fail to purify themselves after touching a human corpse, they defile the Lord's tabernacle. They must be cut off from Israel. Because the water of cleansing has not been sprinkled on them, they are unclean; their uncleanness remains on them" (Numbers 19:11-13).

Anyone in Israel who would whitewash a tomb was putting an outward decoration on something that was anything but beautiful or desirable. Jesus wasn't insinuating that anyone who "touched" these leaders was unclean according to the Law, but He was saying that those people were not helped because of the leaders' spiritual condition—and that's the exact opposite of what God intended to happen when His shepherds or leaders interacted with His flock. This was always a serious problem for the Lord when leaders and followers had a relationship with no benefits for the followers:

"Woe to the shepherds who are destroying and scattering the sheep of my pasture!" declares the Lord. Therefore this is what the Lord, the God of Israel, says to the shepherds who tend my people: 'Because you have scattered my flock and driven them away and have not bestowed care on them, I will bestow punishment on you for the evil you have done,' declares the Lord. 'I myself will gather the remnant of my flock out of all the countries where I have driven them and will bring them back to their pasture, where they will be fruitful and increase in number. I will place shepherds over them who will tend them, and they will no longer be afraid or terrified, nor will any be missing,' declares the Lord" (Jeremiah 23:1-4).

Paul was clear as to God's expectations for results from the leader/follower relationship: "This is why I write these things when I am absent, that when I come I may not have to be harsh in my use of authority—the authority the Lord gave me for building you up, not for tearing you down" (2 Corinthians 13:10); "If we are distressed, it is for your comfort and salvation; if we are comforted, it is for your comfort, which produces in you patient endurance of the same sufferings we suffer" (2 Corinthians 1:6); and

> You are witnesses, and so is God, of how holy, righteous and blameless we were

among you who believed. For you know that we dealt with each of you as a father deals with his own children, encouraging, comforting and urging you to live lives worthy of God, who calls you into his kingdom and glory (1 Thessalonians 2:10-12).

When people had an encounter with Jesus, they usually came away better than when they first arrived. That's how God expects the interaction to be between His people and His leaders. That can only happen when the leaders, while not perfect, aren't pretending to be in a better spiritual place than they truly are. Leaders can't whitewash their spiritual condition. Not doing that requires transparency and humility, but it makes the leaders able to help others who are on the same spiritual journey to wholeness as the leaders. Then those leaders can feed and tend God's flock just as Paul did—as one encouraging, comforting, and teaching example of a follower of Jesus.

Summary Points

- Servant leadership requires leaders to actively listen and respond to the needs of those they serve.
- Jesus' example teaches us the importance of empathy, compassion, and attentiveness in leadership.
- Effective teaching flows from understanding the unique experiences and challenges of each individual.
- Leaders must create environments where people feel heard, valued, and supported in their growth.
- Practicing empathy strengthens relationships and fosters a culture of trust and openness.

Reflection Questions

1. How well do you listen to those you lead or teach?

2. What barriers might be preventing you from fully understanding others' perspectives?

3. How can you cultivate greater empathy in your leadership style?

4. In what ways can you make those you lead feel more valued and heard?

5. How does empathy impact your effectiveness as a teacher or leader?

chapter 8

The Seventh Woe — Talk Is Cheap

Here it is, the last of the seven woes Jesus described in Matthew 23. I've tried to distill these woes down to leadership lessons for today so we can learn from the mistakes of Jesus' contemporaries who were convinced they were good leaders while the opposite was true. This seventh woe is a bit longer because it wraps up Jesus' discourse:

> "Woe to you, teachers of the law and Pharisees, you hypocrites! You build tombs for the prophets and decorate the graves of the righteous. And you say, 'If we had lived in the days of our ancestors, we would not have taken part with them in shedding the blood of the prophets.' So you testify against yourselves that you are the descendants of those who murdered the prophets. Go ahead, then, and complete what your ancestors started!" (Matthew 23:29-32).

Let's examine this particular woe a little more closely. These leaders were claiming that if they had been around, they would not have persecuted God's prophets like their ancestors had. Jesus knew they were denying what was in their hearts and they had done it for so long that they had successfully deceived themselves that they were more righteous than they actually were.

To prove this, history's greatest prophet was standing before them but they would ignore and eventually kill Him, which would reveal the truth that they would have indeed acted like their predecessors. They were going to repeat how their parents had treated the prophets of old by acting out their hatred toward Jesus.

Jesus referred to these men (and they were all men) as snakes and vipers because He was trying to wake them up so they could save themselves from the trouble ahead. They were so far gone in their deception, however, that couldn't even consider that they were in the wrong. They talked a good game, but they could not really play the game.

There are two lessons I want to focus on from this story.

1. God requires truth and will set up circumstances to reveal the truth, not to judge us, but to set us free as only the truth can do.
2. Talk is cheap and meaningless unless it is backed up by reality. These men talked like they were just and fair, but

their actions spoke of corruption, which Jesus labeled hypocrisy.

Leaders must not try to look authentic; they must be authentic. That means they do the work of examining their own hearts, with God's help, to see what's there and then seek the Spirit's help to produce what God would want to see there. Leadership integrity demands that that their declarations match their realty.

As we close our study of the seven woes, let us recommit ourselves to the hard work of becoming the leaders God wants us to be. Let us not be content with a good appearance only, but let the outer reveal the godliness of our inner life. Let us learn who we need to be based on who these leaders were not, and let us hear the heart of Jesus that yearned for these leaders—and for us—to walk in the truth. It was clear that if they refused, then He would orchestrate circumstances to reveal the truth. I want to walk in the truth and not only have an appearance of the truth, and I trust that you will join me in this leadership practice.

We have finished looking at the seven woes as they pertain to leadership. In the next section, we are going to look at the seven woes again, but this time look at how they relate and apply to the teaching role that leaders often have. If leaders are teachers, then when they improve their teaching skills, they also improve their leadership.

Summary Points

- Servant leaders lead with integrity, ensuring their actions align with their words and values.
- Authenticity in leadership builds trust and credibility among those being led.
- Jesus exemplified integrity by consistently living out the principles He taught.
- Teaching effectiveness is enhanced when leaders model what they preach.
- Maintaining integrity requires self-reflection, accountability, and commitment to God's truth.

Reflection Questions

1. How consistent are your actions with the values you teach or promote?
2. What areas of your leadership might need greater alignment between word and deed?
3. How do you model integrity to those you lead or teach?
4. What steps can you take to increase your accountability in leadership?
5. How does living with integrity influence your ability to lead and teach effectively?

SECTION TWO

TEACHING AS A PATH TO SERVANT LEADERSHIP

chapter 9

Moses' Seat

In Section One, we looked at Jesus' words found in Matthew 23 and applied them to the role the leaders had in Israel, drawing out lessons for our own modern leadership challenges. We saw what God expects of godly leaders from what Jesus said the leaders were doing incorrectly.

In this Section, we are going to look at the same verses but this time apply them to the role the leaders had as teachers of Israel. I realize that I am asking you to review the same chapter from Matthew that we used in Section One. But truthfully, have you ever studied or paid much attention to Matthew 23 as a guide for leadership? Probably not, so therefore it shouldn't be a waste of time to go through it one more time. Plus, remember what Paul and Peter wrote if my repetition bothers you:

> It Is no trouble for me to write the same things to you again, and It Is a safeguard for you (Philippians 3:1).

I have written both of them as reminders

to stimulate you to wholesome thinking. I want you to recall the words spoken in the past by the holy prophets and the command given by our Lord and Savior through your apostles (2 Peter 3:1-2).

As we revisit the woes in Matthew and apply them this time around to the role of teaching, we will be able to see how closely related teaching and leadership truly are. Let's start again with Woe One:

> Then Jesus said to the crowds and to his disciples: "The teachers of the law and the Pharisees sit in Moses' seat. So you must obey them and do everything they tell you. But do not do what they do, for they do not practice what they preach" (Matthew 23:1-2).

Jesus said that the leaders He was addressing sat "in Moses' seat." They represented Moses and his teaching whenever they handled the Law God had given Moses to give to the nation. But something was wrong with their teaching—and the teachers. Jesus urged the people, therefore, to do what these teachers taught them to do, but He instructed the people not to do what these teachers did.

Jesus taught that there ought to be a consistency in a teacher's life between what is taught and what they do, what they require the people to be by modeling that behavior themselves. These teachers of the Law obviously taught correct doctrine, but they were professionals. They were so familiar with their material, and so confident that they had the truth, that they made it a "head" thing and not a "heart" thing.

Thus, their teaching didn't always impact their own behavior. It was simply a body of knowledge to be taught regularly and correctly according to the traditions of the priesthood. However, Jesus understood that teachers impart who they are and not just what they know. While the Jews may have been well-informed about religious matters, their learning wasn't translating into transformed lives that were pleasing to God.

If you are a teacher and thus a leader, people should listen to what you say (if it's correct and ethical) but they shouldn't be who you are—if you aren't modeling or living the truth you teach. I'm not insinuating that you must be perfect, but you should keep in mind two things that James wrote:

> If you really keep the royal law found in Scripture, "Love your neighbor as yourself," you are doing right. But if you show favoritism, you sin and are convicted by the law as lawbreakers. For whoever keeps the whole law and yet stumbles at just one point is guilty of breaking all of it. For he who said, "You shall not commit adultery," also said, "You shall not murder." If you do not commit adultery but do commit murder, you have become a lawbreaker (James 2:8-11).

Not many of you should become teachers, my fellow believers, because you know that we who teach will be judged more strictly. We all stumble in many ways. Anyone who is never at fault in what they say is perfect, able to keep their whole body in check (James 3:1-2).

What did Jesus want to see these teachers doing for their students? Let's look more closely at what I introduced earlier from Jesus' discourse in Matthew 23. This is important enough that we review what we know and also look for new insight:

"They tie up heavy loads and put them on men's shoulders, but they themselves are not willing to lift a finger to move them" (23:4).

An effective teacher doesn't just load people up (or down) with information about God (or math or history or theology anything else); they lead people to be like God so they can do His will while they increase their knowledge. They should be passionate about their subject matter so others will catch their enthusiasm and see the relevance for their personal development. Teachers are to come alongside and help people apply the precepts they are teaching.

As a college professor and pastor, I tried to keep in mind that people were not learning in a vacuum. By that I mean they had lives outside the classroom or church. They had young children, elderly parents, pressures at work, and financial challenges. I was being paid (usually) to teach and the students (or church members) were the ones paying me to do so. I not only had to serve them by presenting accurate, relevant material, but I had to do so while being mindful of the life challenges they were facing that were obstacles to the learning process. I had to serve them in any way possible to make their job of learning easier.

So one goal I had for every class I ever taught (or sermon I preached or book I wrote) was to make it interesting. My goal was to hear someone say after class, "That was a good class" or "The time went quickly tonight in this session." I was serving my students by helping them learn in an atmosphere that promoted learning. Every class (or pulpit opportunity or book project) was and is about the student, listener, or reader. It's not about me—never was and never will be.

I did this because I sat in many class sessions as a student when that was not a consideration for my instructors. They were going to deliver the material, jam it down our throats if need be, until the bell rang or everyone was asleep in their chairs. I vowed that if I ever taught, I was going to help my students stay attentive and if they weren't, I would accept responsibility that it was my fault. What was the problem with the classes I sat in where the teachers were oblivious to the state of their students? Jesus identified it in Matthew 23, and it's called authoritarianism.

Most of the teachers of the Law did what they did in part to gain public honor and recognition. They had set up a class system among Jews, installing themselves as the top class! The word "rabbi" translates as "master" or "teacher." There's no question that teachers have a certain amount of power over their students. There is the power of superior knowledge and experience, and there is the honor that usually exists between the elder (usually the teacher) and the younger (usually the student). There may even be the power of giving some their grade, which is their "pay" for work done.

Jesus was making a point that teachers were to work to eradicate any barriers to learning between student and teacher. Instead, the teachers He was talking to had established a social system that exalted themselves at the expense of their students. This tendency toward superiority and elitism, while inflating the teacher's ego, deflated the students and worked against the impartation of knowledge. To address this class distinction that had been created, Jesus laid down some guidelines:

> "But you are not to be called 'Rabbi,' for you have only one Master and you are all brothers. And do not call anyone on earth 'father,' for you have one Father, and he is in heaven. Nor are you to be called 'teacher,' for you have one Teacher, the Christ" (23:8-10).

Teachers need to see that they aren't above those being taught. In fact, they are to identify with students as brothers (or sisters), friends, peers, or colleagues. I don't believe that this admonition from Jesus prevents anyone from calling someone "teacher." But I do think that this prevents any teacher from insisting that students refer to them with a title for the sake of the title. Teachers must actively work to eliminate the power structure that naturally exists in favor of a team approach to teaching that includes dialogue, questions and answers, and honest, vibrant disagreement (not discord) and discussion.

When I served on church staff as a pastor, many people asked me what they should call me. I always responded, "You can call me John." Some people did call me "pastor" or "doctor." I didn't object, but I didn't insist that they call me anything in particular. I wasn't interested in setting myself apart from the people since I was one of them. I often said when I was a pastor that I was a member of the church who happened to be employed by the church because I had a more public gift that put me in a leadership role. That role was an appointment from God and did not distinguish me from my brothers and sisters in any way except function. If someone chose to honor me, that was their choice and not my request or demand.

Now when I teach at the college level, I still don't insist on any title. I give the students my email address and phone numbers. I want to be accessible so I can come alongside my students to help them learn, whatever that requires. I serve them by sending them their assignments when they are absent, returning class work and tests in a timely manner, responding to electronic communication, and giving exams that help students learn (not just try to prove how much they don't know). I tell my students that they all start out with an "A" and must actually work to lose it. I have worked to be accessible even in this age of online and virtual classes which gives people a 24/7 path to the teacher.

Jesus continued with what I consider His most significant statement about leadership in the context of teaching:

> "The greatest among you will be your servant. For whoever exalts himself will be humbled, and whoever humbles himself will be exalted" (23:11-12).

I'm not implying that teaching is a position that should carry no honor or unique authority. However, I am saying that teachers need to work to minimize this aspect of their classroom, corporate, or pulpit leadership. Teachers need to be authorities in the subject matter they are teaching and also have skill to impart that subject matter. When they do that well, it forges a bond with the students that can last a lifetime. Even some of the great leaders in industry or business have spent a large amount of their time teaching, thus making themselves accessible to their followers and employees.

A great teacher Is not only someone who masters the material or develops and hones creative teaching techniques. A truly great teacher is one who serves, not one who has the biggest office or longest tenure or most books or articles written. A teacher should come alongside the students to help them learn, meeting them where they are. The teacher can and must make a conscious choice to be humble. The teachers of the Jews obviously lacked all these traits of a godly teacher.

When I was teaching every week at a jail in Orlando, Florida, I had an experience that made this truth real to me. Without realizing it, I had an attitude of superiority toward those I was teaching. I was teaching once a week in a jail while I was pastoring and working on my doctor of ministry degree. One day, an inmate misbehaved badly and I asked him to leave, which was my right.

A few minutes later, the chaplain appeared with the expelled Inmate and put him back in the class. When I protested, the chaplain responded in front of everyone, "If you don't like it, Pastor Stanko, you can leave!" Needless to say, I was embarrassed and angry.

When I was still angry three days later, I asked the Lord to show me why I was so upset. After I asked that, this question came to my mind: "Are you smarter than that inmate?" Without hesitation, I said, "Of course." And I saw that this was the problem. I wasn't supposed to go to school to be smarter than anyone, even an inmate. I was going to school to be more Christ-like.

I realized that morning I wasn't going to the jail to serve as I should have been doing, I was going to show off my knowledge. That was the wrong motivation. I had chosen to exalt myself and God had chosen to humble me. From that point on, I've tried to humble myself so God wouldn't have to do the job. I wish leaders and teachers would all have the opportunity to learn that lesson as I did.

SUMMARY POINTS

- Servant leaders cultivate patience, understanding that growth and transformation take time.
- Jesus demonstrated patience with His disciples despite their shortcomings and slow learning.
- Teaching and leadership require perseverance, especially when progress seems slow or difficult.
- Patience fosters a supportive environment where individuals feel safe to grow and make mistakes.
- Leaders who practice patience model God's grace and nurture lasting change.

Reflection Questions

1. How patient are you with those you lead or teach, especially when growth is slow?
2. In what ways can impatience undermine your leadership effectiveness?
3. How can you cultivate greater patience in your daily leadership interactions?
4. What examples from Jesus' leadership inspire you to be more patient?
5. How does patience contribute to a healthy learning environment?

chapter 10

Humility

Now let's go back into the portion of Matthew 23 that contains the seven woes Jesus mentioned, again looking to learn how they applied to the leaders in their **teaching** and not just their leadership role. We are doing this so we can continue to learn more about servant leadership, drawing lessons from the role of the teacher.

> "Woe to you, teachers of the law and Pharisees, you hypocrites! You shut the kingdom of heaven in men's faces. You yourselves do not enter, nor will you let those enter who are trying to" (23:13-14).

A teacher isn't to discourage their students or make the subject matter seem out of reach. A spiritual teacher is expected to help a student grapple with and respond to the Kingdom or government of God in that student's life. Some teachers set up boundaries between them and their students because they are scared. They are scared because they may not have all the answers and when they want to be perceived as the authority, they can't allow anything to occur that will threaten that image or persona. That being the case, they try to define teaching as "I have material to teach that I know and you, the student, are the unlearned and must listen to me. If you don't, I won't pay you" (i.e., "I'll give you a bad grade").

Again drawing on my prison experience, I came to realize one day that I wasn't to be the focus of the class nor was the subject matter. The focus of any class was the student and their needs to learn and truly comprehend the material. As I was signing in to the jail one day, I had my prepared lesson in hand. However, I had this overwhelming sense that I wasn't supposed to present that material. I couldn't get away from this feeling, even when I finally stood up to teach.

Not knowing what to do, I said, "I'm not going to teach today. Let's talk about what's on your mind. Who has a question?" That's always a risk for there's a chance no one has the courage or desire to ask and what follows is an awkward silence. Then the teacher must determine if it's time to move on or to allow the silence to continue.

What followed that day was the awkward period of silence when I didn't know if anyone was going to ever ask anything. Then finally one inmate asked a pretty good question, which was followed by another and then another. Before I knew it, the class time was over. What's was amazing to me was that we had covered all the material that was in my outline for the day, but the material had emerged out of the students' hearts and not my own effort or initiative.

And that became the norm for my classes every week after that. I felt like I was helping those inmates to enter the kingdom of God more than I ever had. I wasn't expecting them to listen to me every week, but I was now listening to and helping them. They were actually guiding the learning process but I knew it wasn't them, it was the Spirit of God. And I was just a facilitator and not an expert, not a "sage from the stage, but a guide from the side."

Since then, I have worked to engage my students in the learning process more diligently in every setting where I teach. I have sought to help them "enter the kingdom of God" and to share with them my own struggles, including the good, the bad, and the ugly. I have tried to give time for the students' questions and problems, and help them work through the issues that were pertinent to the class subject matter. For this reason, I seldom have an outline before me when I preach and I'm open to adjusting my lesson plans in class if I sense the students have issues that need to be discussed.

Let me share one more example. After teaching a mission's class at a local college, I didn't feel the class was over until I took the students on a trip. So I took half the class with me on a trip to South Africa. That was a great teaching and learning experience that changed all our lives forever. I didn't burden them with head knowledge about missions; I helped them do missions and then taught them by going with them. Since then, I have taken hundreds of students with me to Africa, some who were formally enrolled in my classes and others who had always wanted to go but did not go to fulfill a class requirement.

> "Woe to you, teachers of the law and Pharisees, you hypocrites! You travel over land and sea to win a single convert, and when he becomes one, you make him twice as much a son of hell as you are" (23:15).

Bad teaching leads to poor learning and good teaching produces enhanced learning. This is what verse 15 is saying. The teachers of the law actually traveled to find converts to Judaism and to their legalistic system. When they found a candidate, they trained them to be even more legalistic and rigid than they were. A good teacher frees the student to be who they are created to be. An ineffective teacher makes the student a prisoner of trying to be like someone else or be like the teacher thinks they should be.

I teach a great deal on how to find one's creative life purpose. In my travels, I have seen firsthand the magnificent creativity that God has placed in each person. I try to unlock that purpose when I teach. That takes time and requires getting to know each student whenever possible and where the student permits it. Even in a large class or seminar, I try to connect with where the students are and try not to impose my formalized material, assuming that "one size fits all audiences."

When the teacher tries to make everyone act, think, or reason the same, it is clear that the student is not the focus of the teacher. The teacher and the teacher's agenda are the foci. A servant leader always makes the other person the focus. As Robert Greenleaf stated in his essay, *The Servant as Leader*:

> The servant-leader is servant first. . . . It begins with the natural feeling that one wants to serve, to serve first. Then conscious choice brings one to aspire to lead. He is sharply different from the person who is leader first, perhaps because of the need to assuage an unusual power drive or to acquire material possessions. For such it will be a later choice to serve—after leadership is established. The leader-first and the servant-first are two extreme types. Between them there are shadings and blends that are part of the infinite variety of human nature.
>
> The difference manifests itself in the care taken by the servant-first to make sure that other people's highest priority needs are being served. The best test, and difficult to administer, is: do those served grow as persons; do they, while being served, become healthier, wiser, freer, more autonomous, more likely themselves to become servants? And, what is the effect on the least privileged in society; will he benefit, or at least, will he not be further deprived? (Robert Greenleaf, *Servant Leadership*, New York: Paulist Press, 1977, page 13).

The question that every teacher must answer is: Are your students growing as individuals? If they aren't, they are becoming worse than their teacher: disillusioned, cynical, or discouraged. And Greenleaf also raises a question as to what a teacher's motivation is: Does it start with a desire to serve or to teach? If the motivation is to teach, then the focus is on the teacher. If the motivation is to serve, then the focus is on the student where it should be.

So what have we learned so far? We've learned that Jesus has a lot to say to teachers! He expects them to not only teach but serve the needs of their students to help them learn. We saw that you must live what you teach, or at least live the role of teacher which is more than standing in front of an audience and talking. Finally, we were reminded or taught for the first time that Jesus is our best and only model for teaching. We not only need to master our subject matter, but we also need to master our study of the Master and emulate His ways in the power of His Spirit.

Summary Points

- Servant leadership involves empowering others by encouraging their gifts and participation.
- Jesus invited His disciples to engage actively, nurturing their faith and leadership potential.
- Effective teaching includes equipping others to lead, not just following instructions passively.
- Empowerment fosters ownership, confidence, and maturity in those being led.
- Leaders must create opportunities for growth and responsibility within their communities.

Reflection Questions

1. How do you currently empower those you lead or teach?
2. What barriers might be limiting others from stepping into leadership or growth opportunities?
3. How can you create a culture that encourages active participation and ownership?
4. In what ways can you better nurture the gifts and potential of others?
5. How does empowerment reflect Christ's leadership style?

chapter 11

Good Guides

Let's continue with the study of teaching as a path to servant leadership that we began in part one. We were studying Jesus' address to the teachers of the law and Pharisees as found in Matthew 23:

> "Woe to you, blind guides! You say, 'If anyone swears by the temple, it means nothing; but if anyone swears by the gold of the temple, he is bound by his oath.' You blind fools! Which is greater: the gold, or the temple that makes the gold sacred? You also say, 'If anyone swears by the altar, it means nothing; but if anyone swears by the gift on it, he is bound by his oath.' You blind men! Which is greater: the gift, or the altar that makes the gift sacred? Therefore, he who swears by the altar swears by it and by everything on it. And he who swears by the temple swears by it and by the one who dwells in it. And he who swears by heaven swears by God's

throne and by the one who sits on it" (23:16-22).

Teachers are to be guides, not bullies or overlords. Guides know where they're going, but must go at a pace that is right for those following while being mindful of the conditions of their environment. The teachers of the Law knew their material, but they weren't servants. They had become irrelevant in their teaching role, making their material (and their position as teachers) so much the focus that they began to major in minor issues.

They also had their priorities wrong, something that happens when teachers get too far removed from those they are teaching. What's more, these teachers who taught others about God were actually resisting God. The very goal of their teaching had become so confused that the teachers of God were anti-God!

Jesus gave a practical example of what they were doing wrong. They were authoritatively teaching something that people were receiving as truth. The only problem was that it wasn't the truth! It was a misapplication of the truth.

As I have stated throughout, teachers (and leaders) must be servants, not only of the students, but also of the truths, skills, or material they teach. Teachers must see themselves as fellow students who have a stewardship and duty to master and serve the subject matter. As a teacher, I cannot help but inject my personality and style into how I teach, but I must not let that affect the body of truth and information that I am committed to teach.

When I stop serving the truth and make the truth serve me (to make me look good, smart, or superior to others), I open myself to pervert the very truth I am trying to impart. While teachers should have a superior knowledge of the subject being taught, teachers must teach students the truth and then the value of it so the student can apply that truth to difficult issues of life and work. The teacher must also teach students to apply truth to new situations that have not yet surfaced or been defined.

The teachers of the Law failed because they stopped being servants of truth. They felt they owned the truth. They ceased being servants of God and were actually requiring that God serve them! Whenever that happens, teachers, who are all too human, will allow their own interpretations and prejudices to be presented as factual. That destroys the teaching and learning process.

> "Woe to you, teachers of the law and Pharisees, you hypocrites! You give a tenth of your spices—mint, dill and cummin. But you have neglected the more important matters of the law—justice, mercy and faithfulness. You should have practiced the latter, without neglecting the former. You blind guides! You strain out a gnat but swallow a camel" (23:23-24).

When I teach, I guide, but sometimes there is more than one path that will lead to a destination. I try to work with my students to help them apply the truth to the decision of what path should be chosen.

But that takes time and creates a certain amount of uncertainty in the teaching process. I must teach the student some specific facts (give a tenth of your spices), but also empower the student to apply principles (justice, mercy, and faithfulness) to the unknown issues that lie ahead of them as leaders.

That can sometimes activates my insecurities because I am never sure what question will be asked, which can cause me to do all the talking so students can't ask questions. When they do, a student may press for information or insight I don't have. Then I must be vulnerable to that student and the class, admitting I don't know while showing the student that they also may not know (although sometimes they know and I don't). When that's the case, we learn together—both of us are students. Learning isn't always neat and orderly; it's a humbling experience. That means that teaching will be the same.

> "Woe to you, teachers of the law and Pharisees, you hypocrites! You clean the outside of the cup and dish, but inside they are full of greed and self-indulgence. Blind Pharisee! First clean the inside of the cup and dish, and then the outside also will be clean" (23:25-26).

Teaching and servant leadership are an internal process, not an external one. What do I mean by that? As I mentioned above, servant-leader teachers are vulnerable before their students. They don't know it all, nor do they communicate that they have arrived in their life journey. They must impart to their students that learning is a journey and a process. This means that teachers must have more than knowledge to impart to their students. They must have gone through some of the inner journeys and "dark nights of the soul" that give an added dimension to their teaching.

I have found that some teachers and leaders are insecure. They cover their insecurity with techniques: aloofness, authoritarianism, condescension, and a rigid style that precludes dialogue and personal interaction with the exception of a privileged few. Yet Jesus, the Master teacher and rabbi, wasn't like that at all. He was accessible and secure, open to questions. He utilized stories and parables to impart His lessons. Most importantly, He was what He taught. His pure inner life translated into a moral authority in His teaching that was recognized by His students.

Jesus had authority because of who He was, not only because of what He knew. He could teach with authority on humility because He had humbled Himself. Jesus taught effectively on love, justice, and mercy because He had processed those issues internally and could teach them externally.

> "Woe to you, teachers of the law and Pharisees, you hypocrites! You are like whitewashed tombs, which look beautiful on the outside but on the inside are full of dead men's bones and everything unclean. In the same way, on the outside you appear to people as righteous but on the

inside you are full of hypocrisy and wickedness" (23:27-28).

The Greek word for hypocrite is "hupocritos," and refers to the mask that was worn by actors on stage. Jesus repeatedly accused the teachers of the Law of wearing masks and pretending to be something they were not. Since they were teachers of morality and theology, Jesus expected them to embody what they were teaching. Unfortunately they did not, and did not appear to be open to change or even the awareness that they were not. They knew the truth but they did not live the truth. James wrote about this tendency in his epistle:

> Not many of you should presume to be teachers, my brothers, because you know that we who teach will be judged more strictly. We all stumble in many ways. If anyone is never at fault in what he says, he is a perfect man, able to keep his whole body in check (James 3:1-2).

The Apostle Paul wrote,

> Now you, if you call yourself a Jew; if you rely on the law and brag about your relationship to God; if you know his will and approve of what is superior because you are instructed by the law; if you are convinced that you are a guide for the blind, a light for those who are in the dark, an instructor of the foolish, a teacher of infants, because you have in the law the

embodiment of knowledge and truth—you, then, who teach others, do you not teach yourself? You who preach against stealing, do you steal? You who say that people should not commit adultery, do you commit adultery? You who abhor idols, do you rob temples? You who brag about the law, do you dishonor God by breaking the law? As it is written: "God's name is blasphemed among the Gentiles because of you" (Romans 2:17-24).

Servant-leading teachers allow God to work on their inner person and then become a guide for others to go through the same process. Someone who has been through that process can be a gentle yet confident guide, drawing on their experience to help others in this learning process. But this kind of teaching is messy as I mentioned, because it involves being personally involved at a level that makes the teacher vulnerable.

Recently I taught a class on how to start a nonprofit ministry. I had each student share their dreams for their organization and then tried to come alongside to help them get started. I recently visited a board of directors meeting for an organization started by one of the students. I did this free of charge because I am a servant teacher. I know what it's like to have faith and start an organization, and I wanted to support this student in any way I could. I cannot just teach a class; I must teach my students and that means I must be their servant. Service is in many cases inconvenient but it is a necessary step that enhances the learning relationship between teacher and student.

Finally, a servant teacher knows history, its proper perspective and the role of the teacher in it. For instance, I teach many African Americans. I read African American history on a regular basis, and try to relate to the history and heritage of my students. But that's not all I can do if I am going to be an effective teacher for persons of color.

I have had to face my own role in oppression and racism that African Americans have endured. While I wasn't actively involved in the oppression, I was a member of the oppressing group. And I certainly did nothing to stop or reverse the injustice. So when I teach, I don't condemn the white majority for their past sins. I identify with those past sins and realize that I am to play a small part in the healing process. For me, that is another way I can be a servant leader.

The teachers of the law had a distorted sense of history and that affected their ability to serve their generation. They perpetuated a false interpretation of the past and took a posture of moral superiority over their ancestors and their sins. But they were destined to repeat the sins of the past because of their faulty perspective and their refusal to allow God to do the work in them as we discussed earlier. They were teachers externally, but were not prepared internally. For that reason, God rejected them as teachers of His law and principles.

So in some sense, a servant teacher is a servant of history in that they must help students properly relate to and learn from history. Learning from the mistakes of history can prevent current mistakes as students learn the difficult task of applying the lessons of history to today. As a servant teacher, I must observe history as objectively as I can and recognize my own role in it all, even if it's through my ancestors.

I end this discussion with a long quote from Robert Greenleaf's book *The Power of Servant Leadership*. Greenleaf addressed the issue of teaching within universities and ties that in with the role of churches in today's society. I think his insight is pertinent to what we have discussed and perfectly aligns with what Jesus taught in Matthew 23. See if you agree.

> The prospect for the servant idea rests almost entirely, I believe, on some among us investing the energy and taking the risks to inspire with a vision. In our large and complex society, a single compelling prophetic voice may not, as Grundtvig did in the 19th-century Denmark move those few who will educate and inspire enough young people to rebuild the entire culture. In our times, the orchestration of many prophetic visionaries may be required. But I believe that the ultimate effect will be the same: teachers (individuals, not institutions) will be inspired to raise the society-building

consciousness of the young. And teachers may be anybody who can reach young people who have the potential to be servants and prepare them to be servant leaders. These teachers may be members of school faculties, presidents of colleges and universities, those working with young people in churches. Some may be parents, others may be either professionals or volunteers working with youth groups. But whoever and wherever they are, these teachers will catch the vision and do what thy know how to do. First, they will reinforce or build hope. Young people will be helped to accept the world, and to believe that they can learn to live productively it is as it is—striving, violent, unjust, as well as beautiful, caring and supportive. They will be helped to believe that they can cope, and that, if they work at it over a lifetime, they may leave a little corner of the world a bit better than they found it. Then these teachers will nourish the embryo spark of servant in as many as possible and help prepare those who are able—to lead!

Thus I do not see the prospect for the servant idea being carried by a great mass movement—not soon.

I have premised this discussion on building hope in the young and preparing some of them to serve and lead. As an oldster,

I have hope that is supported by the belief that some seminaries and foundations will have (or find) trustees of the stature who will help them (seminaries and foundations) to be self-regenerating institutions. These then will become sources of prophetic visions for, and supports of organizational strength in, schools and churches which will minister to individuals and to the vast structure of operating institutions that make up our complex society. Central to this ministry will be the encouragement of teachers and servants—some of whom will become leaders who make their careers as regenerating influences within institutions of all sorts, including seminaries and foundations—thus closing the loop. But the prime movers in this process are trustees of foundations and seminaries. It is for these exceptionally able and dedicated trustees to initiate and to sustain the process. I believe that a few will. This is the basis of my hope.

Beyond my hope, I have a speculative prospect to share that some of these servant-leaders will bring together communities of seekers who find—and continue to seek, thus adding a new building force that works toward an evolving caring society.

Greenleaf continued:

My estimate of the chief institutional

problem of some churches is that they have put too high a priority on preaching and too little priority on being. The churches of today will have more influence on the quality of society as a whole (which means, to some extent, the quality of the institutions that comprise it) if they think of their prime influence as being, through what they model as institutions. It may be that what a church is as an institution will have more impact on its own member than what it says to them. This is not to denigrate what is said, that is terribly important—just not as important as what it is. (Robert Greenleaf, *The Power of Servant Leadership*, San Francisco: Berrett-Koehler Publishers, Inc. 1998, page 75).

As we conclude this chapter on accountability and the importance of transparency in leadership, we prepare to delve deeper into the personal qualities and spiritual disciplines that sustain servant leaders over time. Beginning with Chapter 12, we will explore how courage, gratitude, and other essential traits empower leaders to navigate challenges and remain faithful in their calling. You will be invited to reflect on your own leadership journey and then I will equip you with practical insights to help you grow stronger, more resilient, and more effective in teaching and serving others.

Summary Points

- Servant leaders embrace accountability, holding themselves responsible to God and those they lead.
- Jesus exemplified accountability through obedience to the Father's will and transparency with His disciples.
- Leadership thrives in environments where mutual accountability fosters trust and growth.
- Teaching requires leaders to be open to correction and committed to continual improvement.
- Accountability ensures leaders remain faithful stewards of their roles and responsibilities.

Reflection Questions

1. How do you practice accountability in your leadership or teaching roles?
2. What systems or relationships help keep you accountable?
3. How do you respond to correction or feedback?
4. In what ways can fostering accountability improve your leadership effectiveness?
5. How does accountability deepen your relationship with God and those you lead?

chapter 12

Jesus Came to Serve

We have examined the ability and need of teachers to develop and embody the skills and awareness necessary to become a servant leader. This relates to everyone and not just those considered teachers by trade or gift, since there is an apparent biblical assumption that everyone will function as a teacher at one time or another:

> In fact, though by this time you ought to be teachers, you need someone to teach you the elementary truths of God's word all over again. You need milk, not solid food! (Hebrews 5:12)

The lessons we can learn about effective teaching and servant leadership need not apply only to those who officially function in that role, but also to all, whether they are teaching their children, grandchildren, or employees in a business setting. In other words, the lessons we can learn about servant leadership from the role of a teacher are applicable to all of us—and can be applied in non-instructional settings.

We looked at Matthew 23 in the first two parts, since it was there that Jesus delivered a prolonged address to "the Pharisees and the teachers of the law." In the midst of His stern rebuke to those two groups, He made the case for service in the midst of teaching:

> "The greatest among you will be your servant. For whoever exalts himself will be humbled, and whoever humbles himself will be exalted" (Matthew 23:11-12).

Jesus Himself created the link between service and teaching and since most teachers are leading at least their class, then we can see the natural connection between servant leadership and teaching.

It's important to understand that service in this context is not simply being polite. Carrying someone's luggage or opening doors are not examples of servant leadership. Paul summarized servant leadership when he described the role of the main ministry functions in the Church:

> It was he who gave some to be apostles, some to be prophets, some to be evangelists, and some to be pastors and teachers, *to prepare God's people for works of service,* so that the body of Christ may be built up until we all reach unity in the faith and in the knowledge of the Son of God and become mature, attaining to the whole measure of the fullness of Christ (Ephesians 4:11-13, emphasis added).

Teachers and servant leaders prepare people for works of service that are consistent with the pupil's or disciple's work assigned by God. The focus of teaching and leadership is not the teacher as stated earlier. Rather the focus is the student and the subject matter. The teacher becomes the servant of both.

For a teacher to be effective as a servant and equip the student, the teacher must be competent in three areas. These three areas are described in the book of Ecclesiastes:

> Not only was the Teacher wise, but also he imparted knowledge to the people. He pondered and searched out and set in order many proverbs. The Teacher searched to find just the right words, and what he wrote was upright and true (Ecclesiastes 12:9-10).

First, a teacher must be competent in respect to the subject matter as we discussed earlier. A good teacher knows their material inside out. At the same time, there is no room for intellectual arrogance or smugness, for no matter how much the teacher knows, the teacher realizes there is always more to know.

Second, a teacher must be competent in respect to the technique and practice of imparting knowledge. Effective teaching does not rest on technique, but it cannot ignore it either. A good teacher is always striving for excellence, and that involves matching the correct style with subject matter and the students.

Finally, a teacher must be competent in living out the truths taught. A teacher cannot live by the old adage, "Do as I say and not as I do." Integrity and wholeness for a teacher, especially one imparting wisdom of how to live or lead, are not detached from the truth being presented. A teacher is also a student and should live amongst the students as one who is learning and growing.

It is of note that the main emphasis of Jesus' earth mission was teaching and even His opponents had to admit that He was effective.

> When the crowds heard this, they were astonished at his teaching (Matthew 22:33).

> Yet they could not find any way to do it, because all the people hung on his words (Luke 19:48).

> While Jesus was teaching in the temple courts, he asked, "How is it that the teachers of the law say that the Christ is the son of David? David himself, speaking by the Holy Spirit, declared: '"The Lord said to my Lord: "Sit at my right hand until I put your enemies under your feet." 'David himself calls him 'Lord.' How then can he be his son?" *The large crowd listened to him with delight* (Mark 12:35-37, emphasis added).

> Finally the temple guards went back to the chief priests and Pharisees, who asked them, "Why didn't you bring him in?"

"No one ever spoke the way this man does," the guards declared (John 7:45-46).

While Jesus was a good teacher, He saw that the essence of what He had come to do was to serve:

> Jesus called them together and said, "You know that those who are regarded as rulers of the Gentiles lord it over them, and their high officials exercise authority over them. Not so with you. Instead, whoever wants to become great among you must be your servant, and whoever wants to be first must be slave of all. For even the Son of Man did not come to be served, but to serve, and to give his life as a ransom for many" (Mark 10:42-45).

We refer to Jesus as Lord, Savior, Master, and King, but do we realize that everyone one of those labels involves leadership? Yet Jesus did not come to establish an earthly throne. Instead, He came to serve, to meet the greatest needs people had, whether it was healing, truth, forgiveness, or purpose. And how did He serve the people so He could deliver what only He had to offer: He did so as a teacher.

However, Jesus wasn't the first or only servant leader to be an effective teacher. Joseph, a servant leader who served Pharaoh in Egypt, also took on the role of a teacher:

> The king sent and released him, the ruler of peoples set him free. He made him master of his household, ruler over all he

possessed, to instruct his princes as he pleased and *teach his elders wisdom* (Psalm 105:20-22, emphasis added).

Then there was King Solomon, whose prayer for wisdom (literally a "listening heart"—see 1 Kings 3:9), became a teacher of his people, known the world over, even though he was Israel's supreme ruler:

> God gave Solomon wisdom and very great insight, and a breadth of understanding as measureless as the sand on the seashore. Solomon's wisdom was greater than the wisdom of all the men of the East, and greater than all the wisdom of Egypt. He was wiser than any other man, including Ethan the Ezrahite—wiser than Heman, Calcol and Darda, the sons of Mahol. And his fame spread to all the surrounding nations. He spoke three thousand proverbs and his songs numbered a thousand and five. He described plant life, from the cedar of Lebanon to the hyssop that grows out of walls. He also taught about animals and birds, reptiles and fish. Men of all nations came to listen to Solomon's wisdom, sent by all the kings of the world, who had heard of his wisdom (1 King 4:29-34).

Why is it that these great leaders, servants of the people and their nation, were also teachers? Perhaps it's because it kept them connected to the people and their needs. No one can be an effective teacher unless they identify with their students as mentioned above. Perhaps it's also true that teachers who have to live with what and whom they teach is apt to be more relevant and less given to tangents and futile pursuits.

We see in Ecclesiastes 12:10 that "what he [the teacher] wrote was upright and true." Except for Jesus, many of the great servant teachers and leaders have also been writers (a case can be made that Jesus did not have to write since so many others after Him would undertake that task). Why is this?

First, servant leaders and teachers want to maximize their impact, not for selfish reasons, but to help as many as possible with the information or wisdom the teacher has. Second, writing helps teachers clarify their thinking and presentation. Someone once said, "We write what we hear to see what we think."

Third, teachers and leaders who write have a chance to impact not just this generation, but the generations to come. I doubt Solomon realized that his writings would be impacting people 3,500 years after he wrote them. This is of course rare, for most writers' words don't survive the current generation.

Finally, writing gives the teacher the opportunity to spread their knowledge beyond their classroom settings, and with social media, the opportunities for teachings to expand their influence are endless.

Jesus said, "Freely you have received, freely give" (Matthew 10:8). While teachers must pay bills like everyone else, their teaching must be freely given where the opportunity arises. Otherwise, the teacher may have to surrender some freedom of instruction in return for pay. This may limit their ability to serve and lead.

This is why I personally have invested so much time, effort, and money into my website, mobile app, and as many social media sites as possible. Those places contain all that I am thinking and teaching for the world to access, learn from, criticize, reuse, or publish in any way they see fit. I am giving away all that I am teaching in the hopes of serving the needs of those who read. It is an expression of my servant leadership.

What's more, as a teacher I have found that the quicker I give away what I have received and know, the quicker more insight comes to supplement and augment what I've given. Jesus' words to this effect apply no less to teaching than the rest of life:

> "Give, and it will be given to you. A good measure, pressed down, shaken together and running over, will be poured into your lap. For with the measure you use, it will be measured to you" (Luke 6:38).

I try to teach in settings where the people have not always been able to pay beyond social media. Some of my most effective teaching has been done in prisons, jails, and developing countries. It seems that when I am giving away my teaching and serving the people being taught, there's a fresh dynamic to my teaching that is missing in other settings.

I have also tried to model my teaching after that of Jesus. Let me explain. We saw a reference above from each gospel that gave testimony to how much the people enjoyed hearing Jesus teach. They hung on His words and delighted in His insight. I don't want to concentrate on the content of my teaching to the extent that my delivery suffers or is neglected. I watch the people as I teach and if I sense they're losing me (or I'm losing them), then it's time to stop or change something to win back their attention and heart.

I've observed teachers who made themselves the focus of their teaching and they truthfully don't care whether the people are worn out, confused, overwhelmed, or grasping what's being taught. The only important thing to those teachers is to finish the material. They allow little feedback and no dialogue. They are in control because it is their "show."

I told you about several years ago when I was entering a prison to conduct a chapel service as was my custom every Monday. I had a "lesson" prepared but had the distinct impression that I wasn't to deliver that lesson. When the class began, I didn't know what else to do, so I fielded questions. To my amazement, the questions all related exactly to the lesson I had prepared.

What was the difference? The difference was that the students were more eager to receive because they had a part in the learning process. We were discussing what was on their mind and heart and they left exhilarated, talking about our time together long after the class over. I opted to continue that format for many years after that with the same results. I have also tried to make my seminar and workshop formats more interactive with questions and dialogue so that students can engage the subject matter and I can make sure they comprehend what I am teaching.

Then there was the time when I was teaching for an inner city associate degree program when the director came to me with a problem. She had to offer a class on Black Literature and had no one to teach it. She wondered if I was willing to give it a try. It's obvious that I am not Black and I had not previously taught that class, but since I am a servant leader, I wanted to serve her and the students—so I agreed.

When the students showed up for class and saw me (most of them were Black), they were wondering how I, a white man, was going to teach this material. They were skeptical and I was apprehensive. However, as the class unfolded, it was exhilarating. The class was to end at 9 p.m., but at 9:40, I was still trying to end the class and have the students go home. What made the class so special?

I was not an expert so I served the students by facilitating their learning through involving them. They helped teach the class. I brought in guest lecturers. The students chose the material we would study and discuss. At the end of the 16 weeks, many students said it was one of their favorite all time classes. That gave me a glimpse of how the people felt when Jesus taught. He was the Master Teacher who made learning an exciting, challenging journey.

We have already mentioned Solomon's teaching outreach. People from all over the world came to hear him teach. On one occasion, the queen of Sheba, a prominent queen in Solomon's day, came to pay him a visit:

> When the queen of Sheba heard about the fame of Solomon and his relation to the name of the LORD, she came to test him with hard questions. Arriving at Jerusalem with a very great caravan— with camels carrying spices, large quantities of gold, and precious stones— she came to Solomon and talked with him about all that she had on her mind. Solomon answered all her questions; nothing was too hard for the king to explain to her. When the queen of Sheba saw all the wisdom of Solomon and the palace he had built, the food on his table, the seating of his officials, the attending servants in their robes, his cupbearers, and the burnt offerings he made at the temple of the LORD, she was overwhelmed. She said to the king, "The report I heard in my own country about your achievements and your wisdom is true. But I did not believe these things until I came and saw with my own eyes. Indeed, not even half was told me; in

wisdom and wealth you have far exceeded the report I heard. How happy your men must be! How happy your officials, who continually stand before you and hear your wisdom! Praise be to the LORD your God, who has delighted in you and placed you on the throne of Israel. Because of the LORD's eternal love for Israel, he has made you king, to maintain justice and righteousness" (1 Kings 10:1-9).

Notice that she has the opportunity to ask questions and note also that Solomon answered them all. The queen helped set the teaching agenda, not Solomon. Is that perhaps why she was so overwhelmed? Here was a man who had the answers to her questions, a world leader who didn't stick to a script or to subject matter or technique through which he was in control.

And the queen also recognized how happy the people were who listened to Solomon's teaching. They enjoyed it! She actually broke into worship when the teaching session was finished. Now that's the sign of a great teacher!

In summary, teaching is a path to servant leadership because, done correctly, it makes the student and topic the center of attention, not the teacher. For that to happen, the teacher must focus on the needs of others. And teachers who are servant leaders realize how much they don't know, which adds a touch of humility to the teaching process. This humility allows students to enter into the learning process, asking questions and challenging assumptions and facts. And along the way, the teachers learn along with the students.

As you bring this journey to a close, remember that servant leadership is not something you *arrive at*—it is something you *grow into*. No one graduates from humility, listening, or learning. We are all apprentices of Jesus, continually shaped by His example and continually learning how to lead as He led and teach as He taught. The call is not perfection, but willingness — a willingness to be teachable, to be available, and to allow God to work through you for the good of those you influence.

If you finish this book with only one conviction, let it be this: **your leadership is not ultimately about you.** It is about stewarding the influence God entrusted to you in such a way that others flourish. May those who walk beside you become wiser, stronger, freer, more courageous, and more Christlike because you have been part of their journey. That is the mark of a true leader. That is the fruit of a true teacher. And that is the example our Lord left us to follow.

Summary Points

- Servant leadership calls leaders to be courageous, standing firm in truth and love despite opposition.
- Jesus demonstrated courage by challenging religious authorities and confronting injustice.
- Courageous leadership involves taking risks for the sake of others' growth and well-being.
- Teaching with courage means speaking truth compassionately and persistently.
- Leaders must rely on God's strength to face challenges and lead boldly.

Reflection Questions

1. Where do you need to demonstrate greater courage in your leadership or teaching?
2. How do you balance courage with compassion when addressing difficult issues?
3. What fears or obstacles hold you back from leading courageously?
4. How can you cultivate a deeper reliance on God's strength in your leadership?
5. What examples of courageous leadership inspire you the most?

epilogue

Servant Leadership — Teaching as the Heart of Influence

As we come to the close of this journey together, it is fitting to pause and reflect on the profound calling that servant leadership represents. Leadership, as Jesus taught and modeled it, is not about power, prestige, or control. Instead, it is a sacred responsibility to serve, to teach, and to nurture growth in those we lead. This book has explored the inseparable connection between leadership and teaching—a connection that challenges every leader to embrace humility, integrity, and love as the foundations of their influence.

Yet this is not merely a leadership model or leadership "style." It is a way of life. It is a posture before God and before others. Servant leadership is an expression of the character of Christ formed in us—His gentleness, His patience, His courage, His truthfulness, His compassion. And because leadership is influence, and influence shapes lives, servant leadership is one of the greatest stewardship assignments God entrusts to us.

The Heartbeat of Leadership: Teaching as Service

At its core, leadership is teaching. Whether you lead a small group in your church, manage a team in your workplace, or mentor young people in your community, your leadership impacts lives. Teaching is not simply the transfer of information; it is the deliberate act of guiding others toward maturity—spiritual, emotional, and intellectual. When leaders teach well, they empower others to discover their purpose, develop their gifts, and contribute meaningfully.

Teaching requires patience and attentiveness. It invites us to walk with others at their pace, not ours. It calls us to celebrate progress, not perfection, and to value questions as much as answers. Jesus, our model, taught in parables, conversation, invitations, and demonstrations. He did not simply instruct—He formed people. That is the invitation before us as well.

The Journey, Not the Destination

Throughout this book, we have confronted many of the challenges leaders face: pride, hypocrisy, legalism, impatience, and fear. These are not new obstacles; Jesus addressed them in His day, and they still linger in ours. Yet every one of them reminds us that leadership requires continual self-awareness and ongoing growth. We never stop learning how to lead well.

Servant leadership is a journey, not a destination. There will be days when you embody Christ beautifully—and days when old habits resurface. Grace meets us in both places. The important thing is not flawless execution, but continual surrender. Leaders must be willing to be taught even as they teach, to receive correction with grace, and to adapt with humility.

In this sense, servant leadership becomes a lifelong apprenticeship to Jesus Himself.

The Role of Generosity in Leadership

Generosity is the natural outflow of a servant heart. It goes beyond financial giving to include generosity of time, presence, encouragement, and grace. Generous leaders give others room to grow, room to fail, room to try again. They share authority rather than guard it. They celebrate the success of others even when unnoticed themselves.

This kind of leadership reflects the generosity of God—the One who gives freely, abundantly, and without measure. As Paul reminds us, God loves cheerful givers—not only of money but of influence, opportunity, and honor.

A Life-long Calling

The lessons in this book serve as foundational guideposts, but they are not exhaustive. Servant leadership as teaching is a lifelong calling that evolves as we grow in faith and experience. The more we walk with Christ, the more we recognize that leadership is not something we do—it is something we become.

Remember: you do not lead alone. The Holy

Spirit equips you, transforms you, and empowers you. God surrounds you with people who encourage, challenge, sharpen, and refine you. And Christ has already gone before you into every conversation, every decision, and every opportunity to teach or lead.

A Commission to Go and Lead—And Teach

So now, as you put this book down, consider this not an ending—but a beginning.

> You are called to lead.
> You are called to teach.
> You are called to serve.

You may never stand behind a pulpit or carry a title. You may never lead large teams or organizations. You may influence only a handful of people—but if you do so in the way of Christ, it is more than enough. There is no small field when the work is eternal.

Wherever God places you—at a desk, in a classroom, around a dinner table, in a ministry, on a job site, in a boardroom, or in quiet conversations with one or two—lead well. Teach well. Love well. Serve well.

And may those who follow you come to know Christ better because you have walked beside them.

Now go—lead as Jesus led, teach as Jesus taught, and serve in such a way that the world cannot help but see Him in you.

How To Follow
John W. Stanko

The Monday Memo
Every Sunday since 2001 I have written a *Monday Memo* to discuss topics like purpose, creativity, and faith. You can access it at:
www.purposequest.com

The Stanko Bible Study
I have completed a verse-by-verse commentary on the New Testament and I am not writing a weekly entry in the Purpose Study Bible that examines the topics of purpose, creativity, goal setting, time management, and faith as they are found in the Old Testament. All these studies for both the Old and New Testaments can be found at
www.purposequest.com

All My Books
Are available for purchase on Amazon or through the Urban Press website

http://www.urbanpress.us

My Free Mobile App
You can download the PurposeQuest app from

https://subsplash.com/purposequestinternationa/app

I have many hours of video and
audio teaching there.

My Website
http://www.purposequest.com
has all my video and audio teachings, plus some print material, Monday Memo, weekly Bible lesson, and the daily devotional.

Social Media
I publish daily material on all my social media outlets: Facebook, Instagram, Twitter, LinkedIn, TikTok, and YouTube. You can easily find and follow me on any of those outlets by using my first and last name.

And of course, I am always available through my email address:
johnstanko@gmail.com

Additional Titles by John W. Stanko

A Daily Dose of Proverbs
A Daily Taste of Proverbs
Changing the Way We Do Church
I Wrote This Book on Purpose
Life Is A Gold Mine: Can You Dig It?
Strictly Business
The Faith Files, Volume 1
The Faith Files, Volume 2
The Faith Files, Volume 3
The Leadership Walk
The Price of Leadership
Unlocking the Power of Your Creativity
Unlocking the Power of Your Productivity
Unlocking the Power of Your Purpose
Unlocking the Power of You
What Would Jesus Ask You Today?
Your Life Matters
Live the Word Commentary: Matthew
Live the Word Commentary: Mark
Live the Word Commentary: Luke
Live the Word Commentary: John
Live the Word Commentary: Acts
Live the Word Commentary: Romans
Live the Word Commentary: 1 & 2 Corinthians
Live the Word Commentary: Galatians, Ephesians, Philippians, Colossians, Philemon
Live the Word Commentary: 1 & 2 Thessalonians, 1 & 2 Timothy, and Titus
Live the Word Commentary: Hebrews
Live the Word Commentary: Revelation

Ediciones en Español

Cambiando la Manera de Hacer Iglesia
La Vida Es Una Mina De Oro:
¿Te Atreves A Cavarla?
No Leas Estes Libro: (A Menos Que Quieras Convertirte E Un Mejor Líder)
Fuero lo Viejo, Adentro lo Nuevo
Gemas de Propósito
Ven a Adorarlo: Preparándonos para Emmanuel
Desbloqueando el Poder de Tu Pensamiento
Nunca Demasiado Joven para un Propósito
Nunca Demasiado Viejo Para Un Propósito
Estrictamente Negocios
Biblia de Estudio del Propósito: Deuteronomio
Biblia de Estudio del Propósito: Josué
Entrenamiento para Reinar
Puntos De Poder
El Poder del Púrpura
Póngame, Entrenador
Avivamiento del Propósito

www.ingramcontent.com/pod-product-compliance
Lightning Source LLC
LaVergne TN
LVHW051525070426
835507LV00023B/3315